SUDDENLY
Your Elderly Parent Can
No Longer Live Alone!

Your Step-by-Step Guide to
Urgent Decisions and Getting Help

One title in "The Urgent Caregiver"
Series

By Lee R. Alley, Ph.D.

Table of Contents

Dedication

I thought about this a long while then decided... This short guidebooklet is dedicated to people, caregivers, like you. People who get "The Call" at a most unplanned or even inconvenient time in your life; but you respond anyway. Because it's your Mom, or your Dad, or someone's elderly parent, and it's the right thing to do. You are perhaps the best right person to do it, and as Hillell the Elder stated 2,000 years ago and still true today (paraphrasing):

If not me, who?

If not now, then when?

Preface

Perhaps you and your family had the best laid plans. Everything was on course, on schedule, under control. You all knew that sometime within the next few years the family would likely need to arrange some form of professional or institutional care for Mom. But, for now, Dad was taking care of Mom, somewhat disabled, in their home where you grew up four states away.

Then at 1:15AM during the wee hours last night you got "the call." Dad suddenly passed away. The ambulance took Mom to the hospital for now. Mom was frantically distressed but they are calming her. They are saying what you already know, there is no prospect of her going back home to live alone. She has nowhere to go. Your family was caught by surprise.

Suddenly your family is engulfed by a furious sequence of events that seem quite beyond your control.

Hopefully you're reading this on the plane or in the car as you rush to your Mom or Dad. Read on. We have much to do…

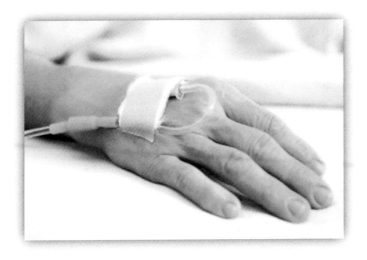

Introduction

I once had to drop everything and run to the rescue of a stranded parent. The days, weeks, and months that followed were as stressful as could be, and I made every mistake imaginable. I determined at the time – that was several years ago – that I would one day compile information that would spare people the same fate.

I later ran in to an old friend who ran a home care agency. I recounted my experience to him. He told me that they had cases like that all the time, that in fact he was at that time already working on a very similar situation.

He had visited his client's daughter, Mrs. Huxley and she promptly broke down in tears. Her father-in-law had died unexpectedly, leaving behind a mentally impaired wife he had been looking after. From that point on, it was Mrs. Huxley, the daughter-in-law, not the son, who put her life on hold to take care of this 80 year-old who could not be left unattended – not even for 10 minutes.

"My mother-in-law was suddenly in my lap the same day her husband died," Mrs. Huxley said. "When I called you yesterday, I had no idea what to do." Then Ms. Huxley continued, "She's here now, with the caregiver you sent, but there is no way we're going to be able to afford a full-time caregiver."

With two daughters of college age, and with Mrs. Huxley's in-laws having – not uncharacteristically – outlived their resources, Mrs. Huxley and her teacher- husband found themselves suddenly staring at the prospect of having to spend down from even their own modest savings.

My friend surmised that while most families manage to cope with the added responsibility, women often end up with the heavy lifting, resulting in stress and often neglect of their own health. As to people's financial stamina, living longer is catching many on the short end of preparedness.

All of this was added incentive for me to write this little quick-reference guide for others. People like you. I decided to prepare the guidebook I wish I had been able to use when my own father, then my mother, died.

Side Note: For the sake of simplicity, I have adopted "Mom" as the vulnerable person throughout the book. Moms live longer than

Dads (by approximately 5 years), and it is more often the case to find a Mom, say in her late 70s, taking care of a stroke-impaired (or dementia, Parkinson's, or countless other impairments) spouse in his 80s. Anyway, for our purposes here, adopting the "Mom" person is better than repeating "he or she" endlessly.

Thus our premise is that your Mom –remember, everything applies the same if it were your Dad- who may live close by or out-of-state, alone or with a spouse, suddenly fell and broke a hip, or was involved in a disabling car accident, or had a heart attack, or developed a cognitive impairment, or is being discharged from a hospital today.

The mere fact that Mom lives alone, no matter how independently minded she may be, makes her more and more at risk as the years pass. Vulnerable to a myriad of events that suddenly trigger a surprise crisis in housing, health care, daily living or nutrition, or all of the above.

Those surprises are called "trigger events". They suddenly compress what you thought were going to be the next several years of age-related planning and decisions, in to a few days.

Dad's sudden passing would be an example of one of these trigger events. Mom slipping in the bathroom and breaking her hip could also qualify. If it's not a broken hip, we could get a call from a neighbor saying that they found Mom wandering in their back yard. (This happens more often than you may think.) There are 5 million Alzheimer's patients in the country, and countless other people with all forms of dementia. Here are some of the most common events to expect (and prepare for!) with elderly parents:

- Stroke or heart attack
- Fall and injuries
- Dementia & short term memory loss

- Alzheimer's
- Severe Pneumonia
- Fire
- Severe Depression & withdrawal.

There are many more, and to cite them all would not change the scenario much.

I find it amazing that these events still catch so many people like you and me by surprise. Shouldn't we be anticipating events like that when our parent is in her seventies or eighties? Whatever triggered the sudden surprise for you, the common outcome of all of these events is often the same:

Suddenly, your elderly parent can no longer live home alone!

My point here is not to find fault with your planning (nor my own lack of planning when I got "the call"). It is to help you find relief!

If you or your family are in this situation, if you know someone who is, or if you just want to be prepared when it does (and it likely will), then this may be the best guidebook of tips to follow (and traps to avoid). Given what is at stake in safety, health, and preparedness for your parent(s), harmony and cooperation among your family members, as well as financial stakes in real estate, autos and financial accounts, can you afford not to have an action plan like this on hand, ready for the inevitable?

But first, I'd like to clarify that this quick-reference guide is a short informal conversation. The one you'd like to have with someone who's been down the road you're about to travel. Please don't expect this to be a thorough textbook of all underlying principals, or a complete checklist of everything to do, not even a reference book for what to do in every situation. This is not a complete manual. Not a training course. Think of this short booklet as nothing more than the fold-out flyer that comes with your first aid kit. Just enough tips and methods to help you get through the first steps, started in the right direction, to feel more confident that there are not so likely to be any major catch-22's no one told you about. You will need a lot more information than what's in here. But this would be a very good first-reference to get you started in the 100 right directions that lie ahead.

And, if you don't even have time to sit down and read this, then at least you can see what help the several checklists provide. You get a few tips for a few bucks for a few minutes of conversation. I hope you enjoy it. I hope you let me know how it goes. To comment, please visit my blog on senior issues at www.ASAPforSeniors.org, and the subordinate material at www.PromiseLiving.org.

If you feel that these scenarios are a long way off for you, as I did the day before we got "The Call," here are some typical warning signs from the U.S. Health and Human Services EldercareLocator.gov web site:

- Changed **eating habits** within the last year resulting in weight loss, having no appetite, or missed meals?
- Neglected personal **hygiene** resulting in wearing dirty clothes, body odor, bad breath, neglected nails and teeth, sores on the skin?
- Neglected their **home** so it is not as clean or sanitary as you remember growing up?
- Exhibited inappropriate **behavior** by being unusually loud or quiet, paranoid, agitated, making phone calls at all hours?
- Changed **relationship** patterns such that friends and neighbors have expressed concerns?

- Had **physical problems** such as burns or injury marks resulting from general weakness, forgetfulness, or possible misuse of alcohol or prescribed medications?
- Decreased or **stopped participating** in activities that were previously important to them such as bridge or a book club, dining with friends, or attending religious services?
- Exhibited **forgetfulness** resulting in unopened mail, piling newspapers, not filling their prescriptions, or missed appointments?
- Mishandled **finances** such as not paying bills, losing money, paying bills twice or more, or hiding money?

- Made **unusual purchases** such as buying more than one magazine subscription of the same magazine, entered an unusual amount of contests, increased usage of purchasing from television advertisements

Assess the Situation

OK. Let's get started.

You already know you want to get to new arrangements ASAP. Mom needs to be safe, healthy, happy, and remain as financially solvent as possible. And you want the family to not have to sacrifice a lot more of those same types of burdens than she would want you to. So let's take stock of where you are starting from. Even more important, how in the world are you going to determine where *that* is?

It is all very perplexing. And when you have to overcome your initial shock and you start talking to people, to your spouse, your best friend, her neighbor who is a nurse, and that other friend who has elderly folks, you may become inundated with advice. And it can frequently be contradicting tidbits of disjoint anecdotal information.

No one can do this step for you. You can get, and will need, a lot of help from various trained experts. But, initially there can be a lot of confusion and a sense of paralysis that you press yourself hard to overcome. This is not the time for getting more and more overwhelmed.

You will get the story of how best to help your Mom from different people, and you will not know who to believe. Perhaps little will make sense in those early hours after you get the news.

The most urgent priority is for *you* to settle on the new reality, which is easier said than done. There are so many different aspects to what you have to cope with. The central issue driving all this is that you have been told your elderly parent can no longer live home alone. Please work toward being sure you, your mom or dad, and your entire family have all re-oriented to that new reality. This is no time to be debating where you're trying to end up. You're going to need to address a range of unfamiliar topics such as:

- What are the most urgent things to address on Day-1? Week-1? First month? Year?
- Where will Mom stay immediately upon hospital discharge? And later?
- How will her needs for eating, hygiene, and activities of daily living be handled?
- How will we get Mom to go along with the plan?
- How will we in the family develop a plan that even we can all agree on?
- What will happen to her house? Her car? Her great-grandma's four-post bed? ...all her hoarded possessions?
- How will she (or we) pay for all this?
- How do we discern true helpers from profiteers?
- What can wait until tomorrow or next week? What must we start on right now?

About this time you'll be coming to the conclusion that you sure could use a step-by-step emergency response plan, and you could use it now!

Organizing **Yourself** for Support

Let's call "Time Out" right here and pause for a crucial moment of self-reflection.

In the next few chapters we are going to be talking about a lot of different people and organizations, in addition to your family, Mom's friends and any number of others. You're going to be wondering if they can, and will, do their jobs right, on time, and with your mother's best interests are heart.

But right now, I'd like you to just pause for a few precious moments and have you consider yourself. You are about to embark on perhaps one of the most challenging (if not also the most rewarding) phases of your life. Just as with a toddler's parent, you and your own welfare are too important to risk, too precious to let become hardened by setbacks and weakened by stresses. You are too irreplaceable.

One piece of advice I want to emphasize as much as any single recommendation in this guidebooklet is that it is just as important to arrange for your own long term welfare as for your Mom. Read that phrase again. Carry it with you for the next year and never let it go. If you've raised a toddler, you know that role. And that type of irreplaceable role is back. Enjoy it. Cherish it. Wear it proudly. And protect yourself just as doggedly as you look after your Mom. She will need that from you.

In addition, in your "other life" you have a job, perhaps children and a spouse, your church, and you can't just leave indefinitely. You worked hard at the firm, and they will miss you, too. Many people, in addition to your Mom, are going to have demands on you as you focus more and more resources and yourself on Mom. But keep in mind, you have to demand something, too, and that is to keep yourself strong in spirit, mind and body. It is fine to just tell people that is your plan, so they can begin to reshape their worlds to accommodate your new relationships with them. You're offering them a "developmental opportunity."

Now, turn toward your Mom and her new world. There may develop a constant parade of service providers coming and going to and into the home. Nurses, speech therapist, physical therapist, home remodeler, food deliveries, real estate agent, and on and on. In some cases on some days it will feel like New York's Grand Central Station. But don't just let it happen willy nilly.

Consider setting up a sign-in sheet and train every cottin pickin' one of them, "I don't care who you are, please sign in any time you come to this home, so I can keep track of you and keep myself together." The busier it gets the more likely you'll have no idea when Ms. Handy the caregiver came and went, and why her employer is billing for this ___ many hours. It can also help you retrieve important points in time such as when certain drugs were delivered and began treatment. This will sound a lot less looney two months from now than it does now. And to keep it to a low-looney level, you may want to use the "Log of In-Home Client Services Delivered" worksheet I have included in the back of this booklet. That way at the end of each week both Mom and her caregiver sign on the bottom line to authorize you to make payment to the caregiver. This will also help provide other records that therapists and her doctor may like to know about in terms of "what has Mom been doing since I saw her last?"

Caregiving & Caregivers

I spent some time as a high altitude mountain climber. Alps, South American Andes and such. Most people don't just start walking up high mountains. Serious mountaineers take weeks to mobilize, and then coordinate teams of widely diverse experts and providers in critical areas such as meals, climbing hardware, emergency evacuation, sleep systems, footgear, safety ropes, communications, and much more. That's what you are going to do. But in $1/10^{th}$ the time. Welcome to "Mt. Caregiver."

We find that one of the prevalent conditions among new caregivers is that they (you) may fail to recognize that point in time when you have become a Caregiver. That happened to my brother and me. We thought we were just taking care of Dad. It didn't register with us that we had basically begun a new career, one with a consuming passion, requiring extensive specialized training and capable of demanding every waking moment of attention. Or thereabouts. So here's a quickie test for you to take from the United Hospital Fund's Next Step in Care Guides. In the style of Jeff Foxworthy: "You are a caregiver if you:

- Take care of someone who has a chronic need
- Manage medications or coordinate with medical professionals
- Help with Activities of Daily Living (ADL's) such as bathing, hygiene
- Handle household chores.

The reason it is so important to recognize when you are a caregiver is two-fold. First, under recent federal regulations (HIPAA), you have a unique right to receive and discuss medical and treatment information you may need a HIPAA Caregiver Release Form, apart from your local hospital's policies), second, you have a right to be involved in deliberations and decisions regarding treatment and administration of personal affairs if needed, third, it should alert you to the fact you will likely endure many of the same stresses as most caregivers, and secondly, there are a host of services and peer advice available to you that you will need and greatly appreciate.

One of your first tasks will be to identify the experts who you need to "put on speed-dial." They will help you build a broader list of various providers and advisors that you will need to work with. And one of your earliest tasks will be to prioritize which of those to meet with the first day, then the first week, first month, etc.

You are likely to have more than can be done in one sitting or one family meeting. Where will Mom live? Will you need to prepare her house for sale? Mom's home equity comprises perhaps her greatest source of assets to pay bills. You will want to carefully select a well-suited realtor who is specially trained as a Seniors Real Estate Specialist (i.e., one who shows a pattern of true interest in working with seniors and their families to sell their homes). For a national directory of these specialists see:

www.SeniorsRealEstate.com

Further, you may have no idea how much money Mom has in her savings account. With one of your own kids in college, you can hardly afford to take care of Mom financially.

And who is going to look after Mom when you return to your own home? If she has a broken hip, it means she is non-ambulatory, which means she needs professionally trained helpers who can transfer her *safely* from bed to couch, who can bathe her *safely*, and so much more.

Welcome to the vast realm of "caregiving", not in a clinical sense, but the way I experienced it myself, and I hope the way it is going to be most useful to you. It amazes me that with so much social studies and public health education in our school systems, with so much citizenship addressed in scouts, so much advocated by churches, government agencies and the like, so very few of us grow up knowing a twit about "caregiving" for seniors. It's a whole discipline unto itself. Partially because caregiving for children can be comparatively simpler, with our authority ("power"?) over the children who live within our own homes. Trying to be a caregiver for your aging parent, however, can be like trying to raise an adolescent child who lives alone in another state with his own means and able to commit to legal contracts. Welcome to the world of "caregiving." You are in for a real adventure.

If Mom is alert, ambulatory, continent, and does not have an illness that requires her to, for example, to be seen by registered nurses and physicians all the time, you can become her caregiver yourself. You will need to manage her household, do some housekeeping, buy groceries, prepare meals, keep her company, and take her out occasionally.

It is not easy. The risks of stress and depression *for you* are overwhelming, If you have to, then you will, but hopefully only until you find better and longer term solutions. You may have no choice in the matter, at least for a few days.

If Mom is non-ambulatory, think "transfers." *SAFE* transfer.

From bed to wheelchair, to couch, back to wheelchair, over the edge of the bathtub, and so on, all day long. Every day. One of the most chronic complaints of untrained caregivers is backache! Even the National Occupational Safety and Health Administration has <u>extensive guidelines</u> on how to transfer, training required for transfer, acceptably safe devices that best fit each transfer scenario.

If Mom is not alert, if she has dementia, short term memory loss, Alzheimer's, she cannot be left unattended. Her entire life may depend on keeping her from wandering outdoors, causing herself harm in any one of many ways, or setting the house on fire.

If Mom is incontinent, you will have to deal with incontinence, and a daily routine that is punctuated by unpleasant incontinence-related tasks, such as occasional diarrhea.

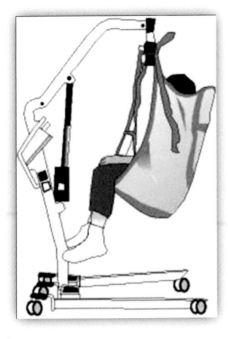

I think you get the drift of where we are going with this. If Mom is any of the above:

- non-ambulatory
- confused
- incontinent or
- has a debilitating disease

…then you are very likely going to need to hire a professionally trained caregiver. You may elect to hire a professional caregiver for enough days until you place Mom in another setting outside her home. But you may well, nevertheless, have to hire a caregiver.

In any case, even if you are the caregiver, it will be best to work out ahead of time with all caregivers, with your family and with your caregiver's employer, two basic protocols regarding urgent care. One is, under what conditions will the caregiver summon 911 (or not)? Secondly, under what conditions will the caregiver drive Mom to an urgent care center or ER? You don't need the distraction of any arguing between any two parties in regard to who is responsible for the bill from an urgent care center or an ambulance service. You can't anticipate it all, but I can tell you from (unpleasant) experiences that this is one of the most problematic topics to resolve.

All caregivers should have easy and fast access to the pharmacy inventory and dosage log (see appendix), so they (you) can grab it take to urgent care or to scheduled appointments. Also, if you are away for respite and an ambulance is summoned to your Mom at home, you will want the EMT's to have quick alert to these records if needed.

Agency Caregivers

We will handle later how to choose a home care agency. We would like to describe caregivers in this section so that you know what to expect and how much it costs. Just for introduction (this is not an endorsement or review), you can check out one of the providers, Comfort Keepers. It is one of many.

When you hire an agency for Mom, chances are the caregiver they assign to you will be a CNA (Certified Nursing Assistant), also known as a PCA (Personal Care Assistant), or a HHA (Home Health Aide) -all widespread appellations for the same level of Aide. CNAs are the backbone of home care agencies, assisted living facilities, and wherever else seniors and others dwell, receive medical assistance, or convalesce.

In the early 20th century, at the dawn of the industrial revolution, caregivers were domestic maids and housekeepers that people employed. Today a caregiver is a trained, vetted, certified, licensed, bonded, TB vaccinated, CPR trained woman, frequently on her way to further nursing accomplishments.

They arrive at your doorstep with different mindsets and from highly divergent backgrounds.

There is one dominant factor that is common to them: they all took the time, about 100 or 120 hours, at a Community College or Nursing Academy, and they incurred the expense, about $1,000 or a little more, for specialized schooling followed by State certification.

By the time your Agency caregiver knocks at your door, you know that she has the requisite knowhow and experience to look after Mom, irrespective of Mom's ailments. The agency gives you the added assurance that someone else will fill-in for your primary caregiver if she is sick or on weekends –that role of filling in is vital for someone like you who was brought into the fray all of a sudden. Your Mom will be typecast as someone who cannot be left unattended, and the Agency will hold itself responsible.

If you're lucky, the person at your door will be a great caregiver. Being someone's caregiver is primarily a giving task. Naturally, caregivers get paid and pursue a highly respectable profession; but in essence, that is seconded to the role they play as givers, or caregivers. As caregivers, they affect their clients' wellbeing and peace of mind in several aspects of their lives, a critical responsibility that great caregivers quickly learn to adopt.

Thus going the agency route brings immediate relief –as soon, that is, as you get the agency going, and as soon as they get a chance to match Mom up with someone appropriate. Make sure you tell the person you deal with the type of person your Mom would do well with, and any other traits you want the Agency to factor in during their search.

A medium-sized agency will normally not have any problem getting you someone within a day or two.

You can hire an agency by the hour for live-out duties, usually for any number between 4 and 24 hours/day. The cost in 2012 on average is $16/hour.

Or, if Mom is totally dependent, you can hire an Agency Live-in for 24 hours/day, for 5 days/week, or 7 days/week. The cost on average is $160/day ($4,800/month, or roughly $57,000/year).

You can also get a live-in for a few days only, as a stop-gap measure until you sort things out. That would probably be the wisest course of action if the plan that is emerging in your mind is to institutionalize Mom.

If Mom is somewhat independent and can take care of herself, let us say at night, you can hire a live-out for 6 or 8 hours/day. For 6 hours a day, you would pay approximately $96/day, or $2,900/month (in 2012).

Private Hire

For someone in the situation you are in when you get "the call," finding, vetting, and starting a privately hired caregiver might prove a steep "mountain to climb".

The cost savings are worth the effort though, particularly if you buy yourself some time with an Agency hire.

A private caregiver with sufficient qualifications might charge $9/hour (vs. $16 for the Agency), and $90/day for a 24-hour live-in (vs. $160 for the Agency).

It would fall upon you however to somehow pay her weekly (vs. being invoiced once a month by the agency), to fill-in for sickness or weekends, and to fall on an honest and compassionate primary caregiver from the start. These are tough tasks, to say the least, and you should not take them on if you are going to end up with an emergency every other day. (Please keep in mind, no matter how dedicated you are to Mom, you don't have the special training to assist in SAFE transfers, home safety-modifications, etc.) By the way, for home modifications, you'll want to have Google retrieve information on "aging in place" and "universal design" for you. Here is a national directory of Certified Aging in Place Specialists, as designated by the National Association of Home Builders. In case you feel particularly self-reliant, here is the whole 165-page caboodle: North Carolina State University's Center for Universal Design offers this extensive reference textbook on application of universal design in products and the built environment.

You may not want to pay the cost of one of these certified CAPS professionals and decide to go it alone. In either case you will very likely be needing good sources of various "assistive devices." If you find yourself needing to make your own home modifications, the U.S. Administration on Aging offers some good tips. See the end of this booklet for a checklist of features and functions to check out in your Mom's home (whether a private residence or institutionally managed home). The North Carolina Cooperative Extension Services publishes an excellent "Housing Safety Checklist." Here is the checklist on Safety for Older Consumers published by the University of Southern California Gerontology Center. And of course, the University of Wisconsin offers the most-extensive 15-page "Safety Checklist for Older Consumers" (I used to work there, the UW never does anything less than 125%).

Also, be sure to bookmark the AbleData website, provided under contract to the National Institute of Disability and Rehabilitation Research, an arm of the U.S. Department of Education. This web site provides massive information on assistive devices, in categories such as:

Aids for Daily Living
Blind and Low Vision
Communication

Computers
Controls
Deaf And Hard of Hearing
Deaf Blind
Education
Environmental Adaptations
Housekeeping
Orthotics
Prosthetics
Recreation
Safety and Security
Seating
Therapeutic Aids
Transportation
Walking
Wheeled Mobility
Workplace aids.

Just as you will want a thoroughly detailed inventory of pharmaceuticals and dosages taken, you will also want a detailed inventory of assistive devices, particularly those prescribed by Mom's doctor in case that is a condition of insurance reimbursement:

- Name of device
- Source of device
- Name of ordering physician
- Maintenance, supply or expiration data for the device
- Date placed in service
- Maintenance record.

Finally, you should know that it is not uncommon for people to go through several caregivers before they find their perfect match. After all, a caregiver is by definition a "giver." Not a care "taker" but a care "giver." If you interview a candidate and feel she won't be genuinely proud and satisfied in the caregiver role, then nothing else trumps that and keep shopping.

If after all this discussion about agency-employed caregivers and private-hire caregivers, you still intend to become the primary caregiver yourself, then here are some tips to help. Please understand, I feel that your Mom's health and safety, and to some extent your own, depends upon certain special skills, tools, and access to other resources. Like they say, "Professional race course. Don't try this at home." If you are still head-set on a DIY approach, then at least try to get some training. If nothing else, it can help you anticipate when you will need to hire in temporary help for certain things.

The Care Giver Health web site lists a series of four training DVD's covering topics such as bed and mobility transfers, walking aides, exercise, patient lift and bathroom equipment. Again, though, let me caution you that "a little bit of knowledge" can be dangerous to both you and your Mom. With regard to equipment, see the description of AbleData elsewhere in this booklet. If you do go it alone, you'll need help, support, empathy, and advice. For that, consult these online communities and groups of caregivers:

- National Family Caregivers Association
- Family Caregiver Alliance
- Well Spouse Association
- Family Caregiving 101
- Parent Giving.

Then, of course, there's the ever-resourceful ElderCare Locator's section on caregiving. I believe we owe the Mayo Clinic in Minnesota for my own wife surviving today, so here is an unembarrassed plug for their book, "Aging Parents," helping to connect with others who have "been there." And the Mayo's other book, "Healthy Aging: Over 50."

Contracts

For the next several days (or weeks or months) you are likely going to be talking with a lot of very fine people who offer their professional services with some sort of customer/provider agreement. In many cases these agreements are drawn up by that person's or company's attorney. That attorney is beholden to the provider who engaged them, and not you. This is certainly not an adversary realm necessarily; but please don't just fall in to the casual, trusting mindset that it's all one big harmonious family focused one and all on your Mom's welfare.

The fact that you and Mom know legitimately that you both deserve good treatment doesn't change any of this. Even though most (but not all) of these professionals are honest, well-trained, caring, subject to some form of code of ethics, and maybe even governmentally regulated, the fact remains they run their services as a for-profit business. And they have to protect their business from worst-case clients (who, of course, you are not), clients who would bring harm or loss to them or their business reputation.

So what all this means is, please go ahead and get an attorney lined up to do a quick read of any agreements drawn up by the other party's attorney before you sign it. And alternately, don't just depend on handshakes and friendly smiles. You and your Mom are vulnerable and need to trust people, but this is the wrong time to be dealing with strangers as if every person cares or knows as much about your welfare or behaves by kindergarten rules. The operative guidance here is, as they say, "trust but verify" or something like that. Believe me, I've been down this road, and my own clients have, so many times. My advice here is not just out of principle. There's some serious scars from not heeding my own advice. Just do it. And be sure to follow up with every one and get a copy of the agreement right away, with both your signature and theirs.

TIP: Create a filing system. You'll need it. One file for contracts with service providers. Perhaps another for cost estimates from contractors. Another for elder-care methods, particularly in regard to the "activities of daily living" (ADL's). You'll be finding your parents' records, too, in some shape or form. You'll want to start organizing those records in a way that helps you deal with tax questions, real estate assets, legal documents, etc. Buy a box of file folders, and a cardboard box to store (carry) them in. You're going to need them. To help ease the daunting task of organizing these documents, here is an extensive template you can use to organize your Mom's records, provided by Mark and Walters of Kansas State University.

TIP: Develop an Agreed Family-wide In-touch Plan. We did this when my father first stayed in his home after Mom went to the nursing home. My brother and I agreed on it. For years, he or I would call our father every day. He lived in another state. I called on even-numbered dates and brother called on odd-number dates. But, we still got "The Call" without expecting it when our father had a stroke in his basement!. The U.S. Administration on Aging recommends having an "In Touch Plan." It might include, for example:

- What constitutes an "emergency situation" requiring urgent response or a family meeting?
- What to do for various plausible scenarios
- Who will check on Mom when, and how?
- Identify community resources to turn to if/when needed
- Update and re-agree on the plan now and then as needed
- Share a written copy of the plan among family
- Recruit Mom to act as the key factor of success in abiding by the plan.

The First Day

This will be your first step toward your coming "leap year." This early foundation is so crucial to each subsequent phase. But, still, more important than doing things flawlessly is at least doing *something*. This is no time for paralysis and bewilderment. Go ahead. Dive in. At least you know that no matter what you do, you're the best hope Mom has going right now.

The assumptions we are going to make are as follows:

- Mom is in a distant hospital (let us say in Cleveland, OH)
- They want to discharge her the following day by noon (typical time for a discharge)
- She is confused, disoriented, and incontinent
- She has lived in a small house that she owns
- She is beginning to feel stress from becoming a burden on you.

Naturally, when your time comes, your circumstances are going to differ in some respects. Our "Day-one Do List," however, is such that you can still make good use of these with modifications.

Call the Discharge Planning Social Worker (SW for short) at the hospital

They are at times also known as Case Managers who are either SWs or RNs, and their prime mission is to ease the transition of patients from hospital to home.

There is a phrase, "Discharge begins upon admission." As soon as Mom is admitted or as soon as you get there, begin the process of planning for discharge. Don't just be passive and wait for the hospital personnel or Mom's doctor to ring a bell when it's time. Ask questions. Stir the pot. Become one of the cooks in the kitchen.

In fact, if the medical authorities begin to talk of a discharge date that is simply impossible for you to line up discharge destination arrangements, then tell them that right away. And if you can provide only some of the caregiving tasks, or only some other duties, then tell them, particularly the chief social worker/case worker for your Mom.

The SW in charge of Mom would have information and an understanding of Mom's diagnoses, medications, and home care needs; she would be tasked with liaising with all the parties involved in a discharge: she would get from the doctor a set of prescriptions to give to the patient; she would arrange for the ambulance to take the patient home, the medical equipment people to provide the wheelchair and the grab bars for the bathroom at home, and, most significantly, she would ensure that a comprehensive and reliable discharge plan, along with post-discharge support, is made available to the patient or their family; Finally, a SW is completely familiar with community resources and helps the family make important connections with whatever help is available.

Note to readers whose parents are not coming out of hospitals: the social worker at the last hospital your parent was admitted to will often be able to assist you just as much: call and ask for the Social Services Department, sometimes also known as the Human Services Department, and ask for any Discharge Planner, and get the help or information you need.

Get the latest information about Mom's condition from the SW, as well as an update of the arrangements that she has made or is planning to make. Get an idea of what the doctor's Plan of Care calls for in terms of at-home care and visiting healthcare staff, such as therapists, RNs, possible Oxygen, etc.

Get the SW to arrange for a family conference at the hospital before the discharge. This would typically be attended by the SW, the RN from the skilled nursing agency (explained hereunder), and the Supervising Nurse from the long term home care agency.

Ask the SW to identify the skilled nursing agency that they normally use, but obtain from her a list of the non-medical (long term care) agency that they recommend, so that you secure those services yourself.

Upon discharge make sure you have in hand information such as:

- What was Mom's condition or diagnosis at discharge?
- What drugs is she on, and what are the ongoing dosages, alerts and warnings?
- What assistive devices are prescribed (covered by insurance)? Has any of it been ordered?
- Limitations on past lifestyle and activities?

- Special diet?
- Are there any lab tests yet to come in that you should check back for?
- When and why will Mom have her next appointment, and with whom?

If all this seems daunting or if you need some backup support for needing to address these issues, then this 6-page booklet from the U.S. Administration on Aging, "Hospital to Home: Plan for a Smooth Transition," will be quite helpful.

Call two or three home care agencies and start lining them up

Tell them, for example, that you want a full-time live-in caregiver, to be ready for assignment the following day (ideally to come to the hospital conference with her Supervising RN), and that you would call them back later for a description for the caregiver that they have lined up.

This is a critical part of your First Day tasks. You will be left on your own if you don't secure the caregiver who, ideally, would also go home in the ambulance with Mom, for bonding perspectives and to hold Mom's hand at a stressful moment. (See the enclosed Caregiver Selection Checklist.)

Later that day, assign one of the agencies, based on the level of comfort you had in interviewing them, and based on the caregiver they produced. If that doesn't work out, you can later make the necessary changes.

Having made those two connections, your task then would be to *get yourself over to Cleveland Ohio (as if in our example)* and, once there, go to Mom's house and prepare it, as best you can for the following day's events. Get some groceries, check documents and bank statements that may be found, and settle down. This will be home for at least a few days.

Get organized, with pen and pad

Consolidate the notes you have already made from talking to people, and devise a work sheet that suits your style and that includes a highly dynamic "to do" list. If you have siblings or other involved parties, this would be the time to update them and find out from them the extent to which they are prepared to help. Start assessing where you stand, even though there are still several missing pieces.

I have included a sample Medications Inventory Checklist in the back. But it's not that simple. The stories are infamous about elderly patients receiving drugs from multiple independent sources. Be alert for what has become known as "polypharmacy." The U.S. Food and Drug Administration provides a very valuable and important online database to check out various hazards and warnings regarding drugs, drug interactions, and drug uses. It is entirely possible that you will walk into a situation where you are the only human on Earth who has a global view of Mom's pharmaceutical profile. But even this is preferable to no one knowing.

Go see Mom

Attend the family conference if that has already been set up. Take charge, calmly and methodically. Something terrible has happened that has turned your life upside down, but you have the power to make the best of the new reality, and now is the ideal time to start.

For your information, the hospital, as well as the skilled nursing staff that will visit, are all paid for by Medicare. You will be responsible for paying for the long term non-medical home care agency, i.e. the live-in caregiver.

TIP: DO-LIST

Here is a do-list style that has worked very best for me, especially when multiple parties (SW, family, caregivers, et al) are involved. Make your do-list with three columns. For every to-do state these three things every time: (1) who has agreed (and committed!) to (2) what task or outcome, (3) and by when? Who, what, when. It'll get you a long ways. Don't assume anyone will just naturally do what you are expecting. Ask them to commit to what you expect and what they agreed to, and maybe even write it down. Then give them a written copy of your notes. And then remind them as their deadline draws near. For most people who truly want to help, this is not hassling them. You are doing them a favor and they will appreciate it.

You may begin to worry, "I'm flying blind here. How will I know when I've basically got all the most important bases covered?" In case it helps, here is my own top-dozen list of important categories of things to address. The message is, if you have dealt with about everything you can think of in each of these groups, then you probably have it pretty much covered:

- Activities of Daily Living ("ADL's"): Such as bathing, dressing, toileting, transferring, eating, medication, bills and finances, housekeeping, laundry (No one is in charge of this exact list, but be aware that some insurance, benefits and government agencies presume a very specific set of defined ADL's.)
- Transportation
- Medical, Drugs (Get Mom's medical records and pharmacy records together. See Appendix)
- Health Insurance (what is covered, copays, exclusions)
- Long Term Care/Housing
- Money and Legal (Get an Advance Directive and Health Care Proxy, perhaps Power of Attorney)
- Socializing and Recreation
- Mental Health, Education and Creative Artistry
- Physical Exercise
- Nutrition and Meals
- Government and Community Services
- Spirituality, Religion and Faith Communities.

The First Week

The "First Week" may tax you more than at any other time in this entire process. The more you get yourself all wound up, the more agitated Mom gets. She requires constant attention, and although the caregiver is there, it hurts to see her in that state. And you're running at a cash burn rate of over $200/day, which is catastrophic by your standards, considering that you have the array of expenditures back at your own home.

The most pressing issues for that first week will very likely include these five things, at least:

Take hold of your own sanity, health, and wellbeing

Please don't let yourself get dragged down by the stress factor you are having to deal with; prepare and eat healthy food. Exercise. And if it's Cleveland, go to the Rock and Roll Hall of Fame! Go and give yourself a break there. It is an established fact that caring for a disoriented parent contributes enormously to depression.

Don't let things (or yourself) get disorganized

The outcome for that would affect your health as well as the family's resources. Keep working from a checklist/do-list (remember?...*Who* has committed to do *what*, by *when*!) and keep adding to the list. Soon will emerge the beginnings of a master plan, and it will be clearer to see, and easier to decide upon, if it is there on paper, with facts and figures.

Where will Mom Live?

The Federal Medicare web site provides extensive helpful information on <u>how to select a nursing home</u>. I have condensed some of that into a CHECKLIST for Comparing Nursing Homes, in the back of this booklet. However, Medicare's original fully-formatted checklist is more detailed and I recommend it. This one checklist is so valuable, I'll provide the actual URL here in case you need to enter it into a browser by hand on a regular computer:

<u>http://www.medicare.gov/nursing/checklist.pdf</u>

TIP: One of my clients living in a nursing home became chairman of their Residents Council. One good way you can assess things is to ask if you can talk with their resident member/head of their Residents Council. Ask if you can attend one of their meetings. Ask if there are minutes. And with resident members in the room with you, ask management which are the most important improvements they have implemented with advice of the Council, and which suggestions they have most regrettably been unable to address.

While we're on the subject… don't just accept the nursing home or adult day care owners' prescriptive policy as locked in stone. Sometimes, if you want a concession from the institution's manager, a prescription from the attending physician might help. I have seen cases where the management policy was, in fact, over ruled for individual residents with simply a prescription (that was well justified, of course).

When we recently dealt with a client selecting a nursing home here is how we went about it. First, we developed a spreadsheet of all the nursing homes within the geographic area we would consider (i.e., close to family). As it turns out there is an artificial cap on nursing home beds in our state's more popular "cities" thanks to a prior State initiative aimed at equitably distributing beds to the smaller, rural towns, too. We then checked on each institution's "scores" on recent reviews by Medicare (see the link two paragraphs above). Then, we identified which of Medicare's criteria we wanted to check ourselves (the Medicare reviews database was a year or two old and we wanted up to date information). We then called each semi-finalist nursing home to ask resident-specific questions such as:

- Do you take residents over 250 pounds? (This is a staffing and training issue, besides transfer equipment)
- Do you accept motorized wheel chairs?
- High speed internet?
- Residents Advisory Council?
- Whether surrounding sidewalks are level or hilly.

Having narrowed our list down by 75% we then went and interviewed personnel at the finalist institutions. Even ate there to taste the food and observe the service to residents. Nothing can substitute for a personal visit. They seemed pleased to learn we were being so conscientious.

While we're on the subject of qualitative assessment of nursing homes I should mention a project called The Eden Alternative. It is "a philosophy and program that de-institutionalized nursing homes in all 50 states and worldwide..." My elderly nursing home clients, and me, have been quite enthusiastic about the ideals and methods of

Eden, not so much as rigid criteria as a general philosophy. As I understand it, our nursing home industry grew out of the highly institutionalized, somewhat regimented hospitals, as a place to send patients who no longer needed serious in-patient care. But the work of Dr. Bill Thomas, the Eden founder, has advocated for a nursing home model for nursing home organization, services and facilities that just feels more soft, more human. I encourage you to become familiar with the basic tenants of this movement. Perhaps use its goals and approaches to support your proposals to your Mom's nursing home.

Here are some *rough* guidelines for comparing choices and costs for eldercare in 2012:

For an 80-year old who is semi-independent, as was earlier described, count on $16/hour for an agency caregiver, perhaps $9/hour if hired privately, and let us say help for 6 hours/day, 7 days/week; the annual costs would be approximately $35,000 for an agency hire, or $22,000 for a private hire; add to that the cost of maintaining a home and living expenses.

For an 80-year old who is totally dependent, count on a 7-day live-in caregiver, at $160/day from an agency, and $90/day if hired privately; this comes to $58,000/year for an agency hire, or $33,000/year for a private hire, plus the above referenced home and living expenses.

For an 80-year old at a middle class assisted living facility, count on at least $4,500 a month, inclusive of some "add-ons' or hidden charges, for a total of $54,000/year.

For a person of any age, the national average daily rate for a private room in a nursing home is $250, or $90,000+ a year.

Let's assume, for example, the assisted living option seems reasonable at face value. Mom would lose the comforts of the home she is so accustomed to, and her mental and physical health may suffer if she were to live elsewhere, but many people make the adjustment well, the biggest plus factor of an assisted living facility being that she would mingle with other people and might eventually settle down to her own new reality.

Financially, the assisted living option has the added benefit of being able to sell the house and fund the new set-up, depending on how much equity is left in the house. Further, the $54,000/year that the assisted living might cost includes living expenses, whereas living at home would incur the cost of a caregiver plus living expenses (plus mortgage payments, if any).

If you are leaning towards an assisted living solution, it is critical that you choose one that is geographically close to you or to any siblings you may have who would get involved. Try to avoid placing Mom in an assisted living center in Cleveland if you live elsewhere.

The best way to find the ideal place is to contact a referral service if one is nearby and, much like a real estate agent when one is buying a house, they will assess your needs and chaperon you on visits to three or four establishments where you will be given elaborate tours.

Powers of Attorney, Bank Accounts & Finances

If Mom is financially viable, then you should get from her a power of attorney. Set up a visit with an attorney who specializes in elder-law, and get her "senior documents" done as a matter of urgency. (See www.NAELA.org, National Association of Elder Law Attorneys.) From that point on you should start paying for everything out of her account, and if you have siblings or are accountable to anyone else, you have the fiduciary obligation to keep good records of where the money is going.

Finally, go to the bank(s) and set up the types of accounts you need. For example, automatic monthly transfers from savings to checking, one or two credit cards with small limits for caregivers to use in buying groceries, and automatic payments to third parties.

It has been a whirlwind of a week, but you're successfully beginning the strenuous, tenuous climb. Treat yourself to a break. Look after yourself. Just as many thousands of others have lived through this with proud success you will, too.

One of the best sources of information for finding assistance is the Eldercare Locator, www.ElderCare.gov. On their extensive web site you can find information on topics and specialists in areas such as:

- Adult day care
- Case management services
- Emergency response systems

- Financial and benefits counseling
- Home health
- Nutrition
- Respite care
- Senior housing options
- Transportation.

The First Month

Often, new obstacles and surprises will come up in the first month. Sometimes it will feel like "three steps forward, two steps back." You may find that:

- Mom has to go back to hospital twice with respiratory issues
- The primary live-in caregiver quit suddenly, after you spent all that time orientating her to Mom's needs
- There was some flooding in the basement at the house
- The money situation is not good, and you need to prepare the house to go on the market
- And more...

Those things happen and, as they say, when it rains, it pours.

If you have siblings who, like you, are caring and responsible, then each time an unforeseen event comes up, you should organize a family conference, by phone if there are distances between you. The chores that need taking care of would be divided among everyone, thus lessening the burden on you.

It is tough when you are alone however or, worse, when you have a sibling who doesn't do enough of the lifting.

If you are alone, you need to organize your own life in a manner that permits you frequent time off for visits to Mom. If this becomes unbearable, then the only thing to do is to get Mom close to where you live and into an assisted living facility, ideally within 10 or 15 miles of where you live.

The reason I advocate for this proximity is not just because of the ease of visiting. It could have more to do with how Mom may be treated at the facility. At the risk of a sweeping generalization, it is some peoples' opinion that at eldercare institutions, the older resident is sometimes better treated if there is "family" close by who care much and visit more frequently. The same goes for hospitals. A hospital patient who has a spouse who spends hours with the patient may receive better treatment than the patient who has no visitors.

Go to your Mom's home town and select a realtor you are comfortable with to give you advice and referrals on how to get the house in good enough shape to put on the market.

I say *in-person* for a very good reason. Some realtors are very adept at presenting an impressive online persona that would have you believe she/he is the greatest agent since sliced bread. There are many seminars for agents on how to sell themselves as skillfully (or more) than they will sell Mom's home. There are so many realtors that look great on their own online web site. But some of those agents are the same ones whose bus-side sign shouts "I'm better than whatever agent's sign on the other side of this bus says *he* is the best!" I have met hundreds of real estate agents and I know that most of them are honest, hard working and compassionate. However, the nature of the profession is that consumers must "trust but verify." Here is a list of agent interview <u>questions</u> I offer as a public service. You can Google for hundreds of online lists of a dozen or so tough questions to pose to agents.

Four keys to selecting a good agent: (1) interview multiple agents; (2) ask tough questions; (3) ask them to put their most valuable assertions in writing as an amendment to their prepared Listing

Contract, as a documented commitment to you; and (4) interview them in-person.

And, (this is critical) since every state is different be sure you know *and agree* ahead of time to the conditions under which you can dismiss the agent, change your mind about selling, or how long you must wait to do it (and get the agent's statement about this as a mutually agreed <u>written</u> commitment!). Some of my more conscientious agent-friends go ahead and agree to (sign) a letter of resignation on day-one; then any time you want to cancel, you just send the pre-signed resignation to the agent's supervising broker.

Here is a nationwide <u>directory</u> of Seniors Real Estate Specialists (SRES) who are specially trained and certified by the National Association of Realtors. (By the way, I have earned that special certification and I can tell you that anyone who has been through this rigorous training is truly dedicated to working with seniors, and not just "selling houses"!) Based on the SRES® Council, their network of Seniors Real Estate Specialists can help you identify assistance in areas such as:

- **Property**: Handymen, landscapers, painters, clutter reduction, Aging in Place Specialists (CAPS), staging a home for sale, housekeeping, charities who accept/pick up donated items
- **Legal/Financial**: Elder law attorneys, tax advisors, financial planners (<u>www.FPAnet.org</u>), reverse mortgage lenders, insurance agents, tax deferral exchanges
- **Personal**: Home health care, community service locators, medical clinics, counselors, meals, pet handlers.

When your family does successfully sell Mom's home, if not before, you're going to want to organize a move-out (and to move somewhere) as pain-free as possible. Part of that is arranging for moving household goods. This very detailed (66-page) book on

"Rights and Responsibilities When You Move" is presented by the National Association of Realtors.

Spirituality and Religion

I had relatively little knowledge of either my mother's or my father's deeper spiritual beliefs. In any case, it's entirely possible your Mom had a very solid, well-constructed set of spiritual beliefs. And there's that whole category of end-of-life beliefs, preferences, and worries. Of course, you want to help Mom (re-) organize her life in a way that accommodates her spiritual beliefs. But there's more. If she was active in a church, or perhaps even an online community of some sorts, then she may be able to draw strength from that group even more now. Try to quiz Mom, check on her internet log-in ID's, and be alert for donations to church or charities. Seek out the social network she had before and maybe contact them yourself to engage their help in supporting Mom.

When my own mother suffered an elderly decline, she suddenly tried to disengage from her bowling league friends, her daily-walking buddies, and even her family. This was one of the most confusing, frustrating and important aspects of our early-response activities after we got "the call."

Be aware, too, that in many cases when an elderly person suffers a sudden decline of health it often triggers more serious self-examination of one's thoughts about end-of-life decisions and preparations. Treat this as both an opportunity and a possible challenge. At no other time in your relationship with Mom, has it been as important to gently ask questions and silently listen. Listen deeply, with caring sensitivity. Encourage Mom to open up with you about this topic and make it a shared journey of new plans and decisions. Here is just one of the many <u>websites</u> dedicated to these topics, to help spur your imagination.

Hopefully by now you are confidently in the driver's seat, even if only just beginning, or tentatively. If the project to get Mom into an assisted living is viable, then you lessen chances of unforeseens engulfing you haphazardly.

Finally, I would like to bring up some background information about who pays for long term care, be it at home or in an assisted living.

The Payers for long term care

The short answer in most cases is that long term care, whether at home or in a facility, is a "<u>Private Pay</u>" situation, meaning that the patient bill has to be paid for from family funds, and not, as many seem to believe, by Medicare.

Mom's *medical health insurance*, like Keiser, Blue Cross, Aetna, and hundreds more, does not reimburse for this type of care; they pay for doctors and tests and such, but not for long term care.

Nor does *Medicare* cover long term care. At the request of the patient's physician (i.e., a formal prescription), Medicare pays for hospitalizations as well as , under some conditions, for the therapists and skilled nurses that visit –post hospitalization- at the patient's home or wherever the patient is. Generally speaking, however, the skilled home health care agency discharges itself (ends its services) when the doctor deems that the patient will no longer benefit from a continuation of services.

Medicaid covers long term care at Medicaid-certified nursing homes. This is a government program for the very poor, and it is administered by each State separately. Generally, the patient has to have a net worth that is less than $4,000 ($3,000 in some States) to qualify. Many impoverished people "spend down" the last of their savings to qualify, for Medicaid then carries them for the rest of their lives. (This spending-down is a risky business which the authorities have far more experience with than you. It can be done legally under certain limited conditions, but get professional advice first.

As a word of warning, please do not forget that the rules for whether, how much, and when one is eligible for coverage's such as Medicare and Medicaid can get extremely convoluted, especially when it comes to repeat admissions, total days' benefits, net-worth (even how you arrived at this year's net worth!), etc. Rather than trying to repeat all the in's and out's here, I will simply say, "Get professional advice" from, if possible, someone such as a Certified Senior Advisor®, or Seniors Real Estate Specialist®, or some other certified and thoroughly trained advisor. If you have to go it alone, start with the federal government's own web sites www.Medicare.gov and http://www.Medicaid.gov.

Keep your antennae up, and if you find that you start getting involved in discussions about home health agencies, in-home rehab, caregiver firms, out-patient rehab, adult day care, then the Federal regulations and benefits, and insurers' policies can grow complex, contradictory, and filled with gaps in coverage. Just be alert, this is not a topic to brush off without serious, detailed attention if you need to at all. On the other hand, it's a great category of things you should be glad you don't have to study for if you don't have to.

Long term care insurance covers long term care at home and at institutions. We are describing this type of insurance later.

Here are 2 of the nationwide referral services:

www.aplaceformom.com
www.elderlink.org

The First Year

After the first month, you need to begin regaining your own life again. You have gone through a major upheaval in your life, so factor in some quality time for yourself between taking care of your own family, and as straightening out Mom's life.

When Mom is in an assisted living facility

Between you and any other siblings, schedule the time that is necessary to look after Mom. If she is at an assisted living facility close by, then program yourself to see her once or twice a week, or more, as would be your inclination. When you are there, befriend at least one of the charge nurses and one or two of the CNAs. Take gifts when appropriate, and occasional money tips may go a long way (if allowed) towards better care for Mom. (Hey, I have been there with three of my own immediate family members, and I will tell you, genuine gestures of appreciation, gestures that go beyond simply "Thank you" go a long, long way toward improved care.)

One of the greatest leaders I ever worked under used to say: "You get what you measure." Well, that means if you tell people what you are going to measure about their work, and then they see you actually following up and measuring it on a regular basis, and you even discuss your assessments with them, there are few "tricks"

I know of that have a greater impact on your own eventual satisfaction with their work. So, let the staff know what you will look for when you return. Not to catch them in underperformance, but let them know how pleased you can be when you return to discover that _____, and _____, and _____. (For ideas on what to fill in those blanks, use the enclosed checklists of institution-evaluation data categories as a guide.)

Whenever you arrive, Mom should be clean, well dressed, her room made up, her clothes in their right places. You want to see all the signs of proper and compassionate care.

Look out for signs of neglect or abuse that are only too prevalent in our institutions, particularly those that cater to Alzheimer's and dementia patients. For physical abuse, go over Mom's body looking for red marks on her arms where someone may have held her in a rough (or untrained) way. Keep a sharp lookout for changes in Mom's appearance, skin color, demeanor, and other tell-tale signs. If Mom is alert rather than disoriented, she might tell you what goes on in there. Or she might not, since our elderly are frequently intimidated and fearful of those who look after them. But when she is disoriented or confused, you have to find things out for yourself.

One of the key parameters of such facilities is the level of training and certification that staff have for residents who are overweight or wheel-chair bound or other such things. Be aware of which of these certifications and training are important in caring for Mom, (just ask) then look for signs they are being fulfilled.

Electric wheel chairs are a realm unto themselves. Did you know that most facilities require new residents to pass a driving test? What a hoot! You surely don't want Mom to walk down the hall to lunch among a demolition derby. In one of my most recent experiences, a small rural center rejected admittance of one of my clients because of the "exploding batteries" in his wheel chair. Truth be known, those batteries were phased out of the industry many years ago.

The best thing you can do for Mom under all those circumstances is show up frequently and act authoritatively, not taking any nonsense from anybody. You are paying dearly in that establishment, and Mom deserves to be treated well at all times and without exception.

When Mom is at home

We gave a descriptive introduction above about caregivers. We would like to add here that many CNAs list themselves with several agencies. What they may be looking for is an assignment close to where they live, a schedule that matches their own availability, and a "friendly" assignment, i.e. one where there isn't much lifting or extremely hyperactive type of care recipient.

For that reason, try to avoid hiring a caregiver who lives farther away than 10 or 15 miles from where Mom lives. And avoid hiring someone for 4 hours/day who really wants 9 or 10 hours/day. If you do, some other agency will snatch her from under your feet, and you will end up with a high turnover of caregivers.

Make it a point to render your Mom's home as free from accidents as possible. (See the enclosed checklist of home-preparations.) Here are some of the frequent types of accidents that happen in the home:

Falls: older people are particularly at risk from falls because they are less steady on their feet and have balance issues. In addition they are often drowsy because of the numerous medications that they typically take. Their bones are brittle, and any fall can be detrimental to their life, let alone their health. Many older patients die of pneumonia as an indirect result of broken bones.

You should remove all clutter and throw rugs, rearrange electric and telephone wires so that they are not in the way, and devise remedies for uneven floors or steps (example: mark those with colored tape to indicate a hazard).

In addition, you should improve the lighting wherever the patient might venture, including nightlights in passageways, and avoid cleaning materials that end up with slippery floors; also, it is advisable to invest in non-skid bathmats for the bathroom, as well as grab bars for the bathtub, shower, and toilet. (Did you know your elderly parent may very well see 20%-30% less light than you? Keep in mind, many of us older folks hear less, see less, reason slower, get cold/hot quicker, have worse balance, suffer worse depth perception, have slower response times, etc etc etc.)

Burns or scalding: as you know, Mom's skin is skimpy and fragile, the layers of fat under the skin having dissipated some time ago; hot tea or coffee are frequent culprits for burns -a severe burn can harm an elderly person if holding a hot cup of tea for 5 seconds.

Burns can be caused by dry heat, such as a hot iron, stove, or a hot appliance, wet heat, such as boiling water or other liquids, or chemicals, such as certain acids. Ensure that Mom is sitting down before serving hot drinks and let her know that you are about to pour a hot liquid, and always check the water temperature with your wrist, such as in a bathtub or helping Mom wash her hands.

Poisoning: cleaning products, glues, medicines, paints, and toiletries are among the most common poisoning agents around the house; those should be locked and kept away from anyone who is even mildly confused or with vision impairments; keep the number for the poison help center handy (1-800-222-1222).

<u>Cuts</u>: sharp objects in the bathroom or kitchen should be kept out of reach; those would include nail clippers, razors, knives, peelers, scissors, food processor blades and such; those should be locked away from Mom in view of her disorientation.

<u>Choking</u>: If Mom is ill, weak, or even just confused, she can choke when eating, drinking, or taking a medication; you should keep small items out of her reach, and if she is at risk from choking, her food should be cut into small bites and fed her in an upright position.

<u>Drowning</u>: Mom should never be left unattended when she is in a bathtub.

<u>Fire hazards</u>: these are risky in a house where there is a disoriented person. Store away flammable materials and take the following precautions as a matter of routine.

- Have a working **fire extinguisher** and place it where you or Mom's caregiver can get at it if the stove goes on fire (to have your fire extinguisher examined, you may take it to the nearest fire station)
- Make sure Mom's **smoke alarms** are working properly throughout the house
- Mom's caregiver should **avoid loose fitting clothing** and, when they are cooking or around the stove, sleeves should be kept rolled up
- The caregiver should **not leave the kitchen** when the stove is in use
- Keep all **flammable items** such as potholders and dish towels away from the stove
- The primary caregiver and all her fill-ins should know that Mom's home is strictly a no-smoking zone.

Prepare Before You Get "The Call"

In this section I'll assume you've read through much of the frantic organizing described in this booklet and now you want to think pre-emptively. To make sure you don't let you or your family become placed in those situations.

Naturally, "be-prepared" would be the underlying theme. Be prepared for yourself, as well as for your spouse, sons or daughters, and extended family. But let's get more specific. We'll break it down to the following areas:

- Planning
- Financial
- Insurance
- Legal
- Real Estate

Planning

We've heard a lot about the "Five Wishes" (Google it.):

- The Person I Want to Make Health Care Decisions for Me When I Can't
- The Kind of Medical Treatment I Want or Don't Want
- How Comfortable I Want to Be
- How I Want People to Treat Me
- What I Want My Loved Ones to Know.

…and also the important senior legal papers. But besides those two, you will also need to have a broader plan ready to activate regarding the topics mentioned in prior sections here. Discuss it with the rest of the family, and siblings in particular, so that everyone is prepared (and in agreement!). You shouldn't have to decide under pressure whether the house is to be sold or not, or how much preparation has to go into the house in order to put it on the market.

Similarly, you should know well in advance whether you would prefer care at home versus care at an assisted living center. And if it is to be an assisted living center, you should have the one or two facilities already marked off as "preferred" choices. Some people even try to anticipate things and start getting on waiting lists. In western South Dakota, for instance, there seems to be an artificial cap on the number of nursing home beds in communities, in an effort to encourage more even capacity-distribution covering rural areas, too.

Finally, your parents' medical records should be in good order, up to date, and the "frequented hospital" clearly marked in your plan. It is always preferable, circumstances permitting, to take an older person to the hospital where they are known and have records on them. Like that, chances are your parent might get the same primary physician, thus reducing the stress of having to start over again with a new physician.

The U.S. Administration on Aging presents this idea for a "hospital kit." Keep it ready to go. That way when you get "the call," it will be labeled "Take to the Hospital or Read Before Medical Treatment:"

- **Insurance** information and identification card
- List of your **doctors**, with contact information
- Emergency **contact numbers**
- Test reports, **lab results** and copies of recent X-rays
- Names and dosages of all your **medications**. Besides prescription drugs, be sure to include vitamins, herbals, laxatives and other over-the-counter products. You can use a "Medication Management Form" to assist you.
- List of any allergies
- Health Care Proxy and Advance Directives. You should prepare these papers whether or not you are going to the hospital, but if you have not done this, the hospital can give you information.
- Other items to bring: eyeglasses, dentures, hearing aids and toiletries.
- DO NOT bring jewelry, money or other valuable items!

Financial

This "senior-surprise" experience of your elderly parent will have presented a valuable lesson about financial planning for yourself as well as for your family.

Gerontologists are unanimous about this statistic: by the year 2020, the average female in the U.S. will live to 91 and the average male to 86.

Thus when it comes to your own financial planning, keep that in mind. If you retire at Medicare age of 65, you may live for 26 years or more if you fall within those stats.

But we are more concerned here about financial planning for your parents. You cannot wait until the last minute and put your own family's financial wellbeing at risk. Plan ahead, create budgets, be strict about your parents' budgets, not allowing them to fall behind, and if they had all along been in the middle income category, let them spend down at a pace at which they do not outlive their resources.

TIP: We have found that the tough part of creating a realistic budget is often not so much the amounts of dollars, but, rather, the categories of expense. We just don't have all the types of item in mind. To help you develop a more realistic budget I will include a checklist in the appendix that is derived from a recent client we helped to develop a budget. Major categories we have used include (the first three, housing, food and medical are invariably the largest chunk of life's cost of living for most people):

- Housing
- Food
- Medical
- Hygiene
- Clothing
- Telecom
- Transportation and Car
- Recreation
- Gifts
- Education
- Crafts
- Leisure Travel
- Pets
- Philanthropy.

Insurance

As we find ourselves now, in 2012, some nursing homes cost close to $10,000/month. Not long ago, perhaps 15 years ago when my mother began her six years in a nursing home, it cost less than half that much. Where will it be 15 years from now?

The $160/day quoted in an earlier chapter for an Agency live-in caregiver used to cost $80/day in the 1990.

It is for precisely that reason that the last two or three decades have seen the astounding increase in popularity in long term care (LTC) insurance.

Remember, we had mentioned LTC insurance earlier when discussing "payers" for long term care, be it at home or in a facility. At the time we said that apart from funding long term care from private means, LTC insurance was the only other vehicle that reimburses for home care.

There are now hundreds of this type of insurers, and the policies one can buy are diverse with benefits that can range from "little" to all-encompassing.

In addition, you will discover once you start researching LTC coverage how difficult it is to compare policies. When other criteria seem equal, go for the long term viability of the insurer, like a GE, for example, who offer a wide variety of options (as do many of their competitors). You may get a policy that offers:

- Any number of dollars per day, say $80/day, or $220/day, that the policy would reimburse after you reach a certain age;
- That age can differ from one policy to the next;
- Most policies had deductibles (typically, they don't pay for the first 90 days of long term care);
- Most policies have caps: they cover you for example for 5 years, with a policy cap of $42,000 (these are mere examples);
- Other policies are for life, with high daily limits, like $250/day;

The premiums depends on your age, and on the benefits you want to subscribe to. People buying policies when they are in their 40's or 50's think of the monthly premium much like the monthly installment on a car. You can get a policy equivalent to the smallest Honda, thus ensuring yourself some back-up for your older days, or you can buy a BMW-type insurance, covering many more contingencies.

Don't go much beyond age 50-55 without examining LTC insurance. We give you some links in the next chapter on how to go about finding an independent agent. LTC insurance is definite worthwhile.

Legal

We provide here, in summary form, a listing of <u>some</u> of the many documents you may want to line up ahead of time to protect yourself as well as your parent(s). Don't forget the National Association of Elder Law Attorneys has a national directory of members at www.NAELA.org. In addition, the Financial Planning Association has a nationwide directory of members at www.FPAnet.org.

<u>Estate Planning:</u> whether you have a small or substantial net worth, estate planning allows you to leave to individuals of your choice whatever you have to leave after your demise. It permits you to save on taxes and Probate court, and attorneys' fees, and avoids unnecessary burdens to the people you love.

Your Estate Planning should include a Durable Power of Attorney a Will, and other "senior legal documents".

<u>Guardianship:</u> (in some States this is referred to as conservatorship). If your parents have not already appointed you formally as their guardian and you get "the call", and the surviving parent is still not incapacitated, then this is the first document you should rush and get executed.

The guardian is legally empowered to act on behalf of the other person in all matters of finance, medical, and legal, and they can be any member of the family, a friend, or an attorney.

When a full guardianship is too broad a power to give to some-one, then a Durable Power of Attorney may be sufficient.

Durable Power of Attorney: With this instrument you appoint the person of your choice to manage your affairs, including your financial affairs, if you get incapacitated for any reason, or after your death. If you don't have this instrument and you get incapacitated, the court would have to appoint a guardian or conservator. This need not be the person you would have wanted, and the process takes time and costs money.

Will: your will appoints the Executor of your choice who is the legal representative that you want to carry out your wishes upon your death. It also is your directive as to who should receive each of your assets after your death.

Living Will: How you want to be treated if terminally ill or permanently unconscious.

Medical Power of Attorney ("Health-Care Proxy"): Names the individual who is designated to make health care decisions on your behalf

Universal Do Not Resuscitate Order: Be aware there are different forms of this kind of order, depending upon whether you are in the hospital or at a roadway accident scene.

Advance Health Care Directive: Regards "end of life" issues. See the Five Wishes mentioned earlier.

As you may well imagine, there is more to the law than we have represented here. In addition to "the law" there are numerous Federal guidelines and local hospital protocols that may apply. Talk with your physician, attorney and/or at least to get started, a Certified Senior Advisor®. We have given you links to more appropriate resources in all the primary fields touched upon in this book. My purpose has been to "gently jolt you" to the need to avoid procrastination and get all these matters taken care of now so as to avoid burdening your own caregiver with these tough choices later on.

Real Estate

Real estate for seniors is different! Any one in their 50's or above contemplating purchase or sale of primary residence, or a vacation home, investment property such as land or a business, needs to first do some critical homework. That is because all that prior experience in real estate you feel so confident about, all those early successes in real estate, simply do not prepare you for how much the same old rules affect us very differently when we reach our 50's. Partly because we and our personal circumstances have changed, partly because of what we've done in the past, and partly because we are about to undergo some great transitions around retirement time. Now approaching 70 myself, it still amazes me how life, school, family, business, have such a blind spot in preparation for "the five elderly-issues" (planning, finance, insurance, legal, real estate).

Please, do your homework! The life-exam questions don't change, but the correct answers certainly do.

The real estate industry, the market, and even the homes themselves discriminate with elderly people. It is not all illegal, nor even a conspiracy. In fact it can be a benefit in that certain opportunities are available only for seniors (such as the reverse mortgage for those 62 and older). While younger professionals tend to be high-income/lower net worth, we older folks tend to be the opposite after retirement, low-income/high net worth. That presents different opportunities, risks and burdens than for a middle aged couple raising a teenager and two kids paying college tuition.

There are about six categories of rules that affect real estate transactions differently for those of us over 55:

- Taxation and taxable transactions
- Transfer of homeownership to others
- Health, safety and medical support
- Insurance
- Financing
- Home physical design.

Unless you are specially trained in both real estate (law, finance, architectural features, functional systems) and senior-care, I strongly suggest you seek the support of a nationally certified Seniors Real Estate Specialist® or a Certified Senior Advisor®. (Google either title.) Either of those specialists is trained to help you identify candidate CPA's, realtors, home-health and caregiver professionals, insurance agents, financial planners and home remodelers (for aging in place/Universal Design).

One thing I suggest you keep in mind, though. And that is to remain your own general contractor. That is, keep yourself at the top of the coordinating hierarchy. The one in charge of coordinating it all. You'll be very fortunate if you can be the one on top of the ball, delegating responsibilities and securing commitments of outcomes from various specialists. Like they say, if you're one of the trees you don't see the forest.

Recap

First and foremost, you learned that news of calamitous nature can spring at you from nowhere. In hindsight you may feel you should have foreseen that your parents were at risk, that one of them could suddenly become stranded at home alone, and maybe you could have been better prepared.

But don't be too hard on yourself since a) it is quite common for adult children in their 40's, 50's, and 60's not to be thinking too much about what may happen when a parent suffers a sudden change, and b) you sprang into action and did what you had to do.

In retrospect, you are nothing short of a heroine! *You* were there for your Mom, braving the uncertain world that you fell into. Most importantly, Mom would be proud of you.

Balanced between home and assisted living

You learned the pros and cons of home vs. assisted living. Home is always better, but it can be problematic and ends up being some 30% – 50% more expensive if full-time caregivers are needed. My family slid down this slippery slope of costs until we wound up spending big time for an electric winch/lift on a ceiling track , which then called for an auto-start backup generator, then eventually a live-n 24x7 CNA.

With assisted living facilities, as with "independent" living and other institutions, the risk of ill treatment and abuse –even "casual" abuse (including neglect due to work overload or just plain incompetence or dedication)- cannot be ignored, and you learned how to keep a sharp eye for that.

Generally speaking, if your parent is alert but physically dependent, like someone who is only "frail", keeping them at home, where they have probably lived a long time, is much better.

When you visit an assisted living facility, you will note that one of their talking points has to do with the "socializing" that the patient can participate in. That is frequently true, in that some patients thrive in that environment. They make friends, and at times they even "pair up".

After you read over this short booklet please let me know how you think we should improve the next edition.

And even more importantly, the first time you or one of your friends or family uses this, please let me know how it goes for you and how it turns out for your parent. Send me your story. I'd love to see it.

Best wishes to you, to your parent(s) and to your family.

-Lee Alley

CHECKLIST:
Are You Cut Out for Caregiving?

Are you a nurturer?

What in your background supports being a nurturer?

Do you have any unresolved and deep-seated anger over how the potential care recipient treated you as a child, teenager, or adult?

Were you physically or sexually abused by the potential care recipient?

How is your health and stamina? Do you have the energy to be a principal caregiver?

What is your prime motivation for caregiving - guilt, family obligations, or love?

What duty and obligation do you believe you have to the potential care recipient?

Have you rid yourself of emotional baggage and owned your vulnerability?

Can you express your feelings and your opinions even when they are unpopular?

Can you comfort friends and family members even when they are in distress?

How well have you cared for yourself in your life? Do you know your limits, and do you honor them?

Do you respect your priority needs and seek to get them met?

Do you know how to relax and mitigate stress? Do you actively incorporate wellness activities in your life? How well do you take care of yourself? Are you last on the priority rung?

What role do religion and spirituality play in your life? is it an anchor and a support for you?

How well would your family and home handle the addition of a parent or grandparent?

Do you work at home? your workspace separated from living space?

What kind of financial support can you provide?

Can you take on the responsibility of home care? Are you willing to do this?

Is your home compatible with the potential care recipient's current and future needs?

Can you afford to remodel if necessary?

What sorts of support systems exist in your community and county to help you with caregiving?

Can you easily ask for help if you require it?

Can you set and maintain boundaries?

CHECKLIST:
Log of In-Home Client Services Delivered

For the week of _____ through _____ .

This is adapted from an actual client-services/ billing sheet used by an in-home care agency. In its most useful form, this is a spreadsheet, with one column for each day of the week and one row for each of the service categories below. You should add and edit your own service categories. (The list of services will evolve at least monthly!) At the end of the week both the hired caregiver and her client (your Mom) signs and dates it.

Companionship Care

Assist with Correspondence
Pick up medication
Errands/ shopping
TV - movies - games – books
Transport to Dr. Appt. church - events

Personal Care

Bed bath/ Sponge bath
Shower/ tub bath
Hair care (shampoo. dry, comb/ brush) Brush teeth
Shave
Nail care (clean and file)
Skin care (apply lotion)

Assist with dressing
Medication reminders

Nutrition

Plan and prepare meals/ snacks Grocery shopping / monitor aging food -Assist with feeding
Monitor diet and eating habits
Encourage fluids
Clean up/ wash dishes

Toilet Assistance

Assist to bathroom
Assist at bedside commode
Assist w/ urinal – bedpan
Incontinence care (Depends)

Mobility Assistance

Assist with walking
Turn position in bed
Transferring assistance
Assist with Exercise/ range of motion

Support Service

Wash clothes - put away
Make bed. Wash and change linens
Vacuum - sweep floors
Clean bathroom (wipe down)
Dust Furniture
Feed/ water for pet
Change litter box
Water plants

CHECKLIST:
Contractors You May Need to Help Prepare a Home for Sale

Certified Aging in Place Specialists (CAPS)

Charities accepting donations of furniture, clothing, household goods

Clutter-reduction/Storage Systems Experts

CPA's & money managers

Elder law attorneys (wills, trusts, estates, power of attorney, advance directives)

Financial planners, experts on pensions, retirement accounts

Handymen

Housekeeping services

Insurance agents

Interior staging specialists

Landscapers

Painters

Real estate agent

Reverse mortgage lenders and counselors

Senior moving specialists

Tax specialist (Income tax, 1031 Exchanges, Reverse Mortgages)

Title/escrow companies

CHECKLIST:
Local Services You May Need to Contact in a Rush

Adult Day Care

Caregiver Programs

Case Management

Community services

Dog walkers & pet sitters

Elder Abuse Prevention Programs

Emergency Response Systems

Employment Services

Financial Assistance

Grief counselors

Home Health Services

Home Modification

Home Repair

Hospitals and clinics

Information and Referral/Assistance

Legal Assistance

Meals on Wheels

Senior Move Manger

Nutrition Services

Personal Care

Pet boarding

Public benefits offices

Respite Care

Senior Center Programs
Senior Housing Options
Transitional services
Urgent Care Centers (See CHECKLIST)
Volunteer opportunities

CHECKLIST:
Some Items to Check for in Home Modification Survey

Appliances, Kitchen, Bathroom

Are cabinet doorknobs easy to use?

Are stove controls easy to use and clearly marked?

Are faucets easy to use?

Are there grab bars where needed?

Are all appliances and utensils conveniently and safely located?

Can the oven and refrigerator be opened easily?

Can you sit down while working?

Can you get into and out of the bathtub or shower easily?

Is the kitchen counter height and depth comfortable for you?

Is the water temperature regulated to prevent scalding or burning?

Would you benefit from having convenience items, such as a handheld showerhead, a garbage disposal, or a trash compactor?

Doors, Windows

Are your doors and windows easy to open and close?

Are your door locks sturdy and easy to operate?

Are your doors wide enough to accommodate a walker or wheelchair?

Do your doors have peepholes or viewing?

Electrical Outlets, Switches, Safety Devices

Are light or power switches easy to turn on and off?
Are electrical outlets easy to reach?
Are the electrical outlets properly grounded to prevent shocks?
Are your extension cords in good condition?
Can you hear the doorbell in every part of the house?
Do you have smoke detectors throughout your home?
Do you have an alarm system?
Is the telephone readily available for emergencies?
Would you benefit from having an assistive device to make it easier to hear and talk on the telephone?

Floors

Are all of the floors in your home on the same level?
Are steps up and down marked in some way?
Are all floor surfaces safe and covered with non-slip or non-skid materials?
Do you have scatter rugs or doormats that could be hazardous?

Hallways, Steps, Stairways

Are hallways and stairs in good condition?
Do all of your hallways and stairs have smooth, safe surfaces?
Do your stairs have steps that are big enough for your whole foot?
Do you have handrails on both sides of the stairway?
Are your stair rails wide enough for you to grasp them securely?
Would you benefit from building a ramp to replace the stairs or steps inside or outside of your home?

Closets, Storage Spaces

Are your closets and storage areas conveniently located?

Are your closet shelves too high?

Can you reach items in the closet easily?

Do you have enough storage space?

Have you gotten the maximum use out of the storage space you have, including saving space with special closet shelf systems and other products?

Lighting, Ventilation

Do you have night lights where they are needed?

Is the lighting in each room sufficient for the use of the room?

Is the lighting bright enough to ensure safety?

Is each room well-ventilated with good air circulation?

CHECKLIST:
Urgent Care Facility

No matter how or where your Mom is housed, if it is outside a professional medical facility you will want to have pre-identified how and where you or your caregiver will access urgent care of all hours, holidays, for just about any reason. Here are some information to collect ahead of time.

Name and address
Emergency phone number, 24x7x365
Address
What is the transit time during low traffic, high traffic?
Is a snow-plowed road a likely issue in winter?
Which services are available during which hours?
Are there better times than others to visit?
Check that your insurance will be handled there
Is there an affiliated pharmacy?
Does your Mom's doctor have any advice about selecting this center? Her health insurer(s)?
What are the referral arrangements to the major local hospital and other/specialized urgent care services

CHECKLIST:
Common Household Expenses to Budget For

Housing

Mortgage
Insurance
Property Taxes
Heat/A/C,Trash
Membership/Snow
Home Maintenance
Cleaning Supplies
Garden/Landscape
Appliance R&R
Remodel

_____Total

Food

Basic Food
Booze
Snacks
Restaurants

_____Total

Health

Insurance Premiums
Long Term Care
Drugs
Eyes & Eyeware
Dentist
Co-Pays

_____Total

Telecom

Phone
Internet
Satellite Radio
Cable TV

_____Total

Hygiene

Toiletries
Cosmetics
Hairstylist/Barbars

_____Total

Automobiles

Car #1
Gas & Oil
Maintenance
Depreciation
Insurance

____Total

Recreation

Plane
Magazine Sub's
Entertainment
Radio & Music Sub's
Memberships

____Total

Gifts

Christmas
Birthdays

____Total

Education

Son's Scholarship

____Total

Crafts

Craft-1
Craft-2

____Total

Leisure Travel

____Total

Clothing

_____Total

Pets

Vet / Shots
Kennels
Food

_____Total

Philanthropy

_____Total

Grand Total_____

CHECKLIST:
Medications Inventory

It is possible your Mom has been receiving various drugs from multiple sources. Collect labels from opened and unopened pill bottles around the house. Contact the pharmacies. Start a spreadsheet with one row for each drug, and something like this information below for each one. Keep this list where you and all caregivers can get to it quickly so they can take it with them to urgent care and scheduled appointments.

You may also want to augment this inventory of drugs with a separate log-sheet to record doses taken.

Medication name (Both patent and generic names)
How many pills on hand
Dosage instructions (units)
Dosage instructions (times of day, days of week, conditions to trigger use)
What does it treat?
Which other chemicals/drugs does the label say to avoid concurrently?
Treatment start date
Prescription fill date
Expiration date
Number of remaining refills
Is any concomitant symptom monitoring specified? Side effects?

Prescribing doctor's name

Doctor's phone number/fax number

Pharmacy name and phone number

Is there an ongoing payment account for this prescription?

About the Author

Everybody has "a story." Here's mine. It helps explain why I care about this topic.

About fifteen years ago I was living in Washington, D.C. and, it seemed, airports. My only sibling, Don, lived in Kansas. Mom and Dad, both of them healthy, happy and active, lived in a suburban single family home in Missouri.

One day Don and I got "the call." Our seventy-something mother had fallen, broke her hip. Our father, in his eighties, found her lying on the kitchen floor in great pain. And further, something simultaneously triggered some mysterious and serious emotional decline. Mom had never stopped smiling and giggling as long as I knew her. But in coming weeks various psychiatrists, physicians, neurologists, about every ___ologist across town examined Mom and tried unsuccessfully to treat her deep despairing depression. Clearly, our father could no longer provide for Mom who lived six more years in a nursing home, with worsening Parkinson's Disease... until...

Six years later, Don and I got "the call" again. Dad had fallen in his shop in the basement of his home. Apparently from a ministroke. He had driven himself to the ER, where he immediately suffered a much more serious stroke. He would never be able to return to the home, even with special medical attendants.

Then, in 2011 we got "the call" a third time! It was my father-in-law, Paul, in his eighties, who was several years in to a MS diagnosis. And as this experience shows, no book can prepare you for everything.

Paul had been living at home in Cincinnati for years with his wife, Jane, as full time caregiver. It had become clear Paul must move to a skilled-care nursing home within a few months. He and the family arranged for Paul to move to a Reno, NV nursing home, while wife Jane would move in with a middle-aged daughter who lived in Reno. The family made enormous arrangements. Selling the Cincinnati home. Shipping a 200-lb electric wheel chair. Shipping a handicap-modified van with hydraulic ramp and other retrofits. Medical teams on both ends began transferring massive medical records. And a private medical flight from Cincinnati to Reno (Paul could not medically tolerate the trip vie road in any type vehicle.) The entire operation was thoroughly organized to the last detail like a military campaign.

Then we got "the call." But not what you think. With just a few days until "launch" the middle-aged daughter suddenly, unexpectedly passed away.

We all agreed Jane, in her eighties, was not going to live alone in a strange city, while her husband moved in to a new nursing home. Besides the planned move of Paul and wife Jane, we now had unexpected family grieving and funeral arrangements to attend to.

We held a family meeting, of sorts (more like a panic attack). We had about ten minutes to decide the entire transfer would have to move forward exactly as planned, but for one change. The charter flight was fixed, the handicap van was already headed west, as was the wheel chair also enroute. Medical records were packaged up, ready to send. We invented Plan-B. Jane would move in with us in South Dakota 1,200 miles from Reno.

Now, this is not trivial. Most nursing homes in South Dakota have waiting lists. On top of that, Paul requires certain special capabilities of a nursing home, such as his over-weight (over 250-pounds, an issue for CAN's to transfer him), his wheel chair, and his need to be close to emergency acute care. We quickly surveyed every nursing home for 200 miles around, and found one 150 miles away in Wyoming that had capabilities and vacancy. So we diverted all transport operations and medical-care handoffs to Gillete, Wyoming instead of Reno.

In case you are wondering, it all has turned out generally OK. The family came together in grieving the loss of the daughter, all the family members and contractors cooperated marvelously (with some extraordinary "coordinative" direction by Jane, and Paul was a great spirit through it all.

As you can see not once but *three* times I have experienced first-hand the chaos that follows "the call." We had to go through everything in this booklet, and a *lot* more. The first two times it was before Amazon on the Internet, before eBooks, before federally organized senior-care locators on the web, and before "senior planning" had converged in time with the aging of the Baby Boomers.

Now some details about my professional credentials and personal life:

I am a grandfather, husband, hiker, packgoat trainer, Certified Senior Advisor ®, Seniors Real Estate Specialist ®, and member of the National Financial Planning Association ®. I work with area nursing homes, senior centers and a community seniors-services planning initiative funded by the Rapid City Council.

I hold college degrees in physics, computer science and statistics, and my Ph.D. from University of Nebraska is in management systems engineering with a research emphasis in organizational psychology. I enjoyed a decades-long career as professor followed by senior university leadership roles such as vice president of technology for the statewide university systems of Wisconsin, Nevada and South Dakota. I co-founded a university laboratory and clinic for biocybertetics (computerized mobility and communications prosthetics), then went into management systems consulting. For the past 15 years I have been an active real estate investor and business analyst. I tried retirement, but failed. For the past several years I have been pursuing a passion for serving seniors, baby boomers, and their elderly parents in the areas of caregiving, real estate, and senior-planning. In my spare time I have spent several years raising and training pack goats (www.BlackHillsPackGoats). I am past president of the Black Hills' honey bee club (www.WannaBeeClub.org and http://www.Leez.Bz). I also organized and lead the very popular Black Hills Explorers, an informal club devoted to learning, exploration and hiking around South Dakota's Black Hills (www.BlackHillsExplorers.org). My blogs for seniors real estate are at www.Promise-Living.org and ActiveRain.com/blogs/LeeAlley. I developed a free public service website for the consumer public to directly access a complete and daily-updated copy of the same Black Hills MLS data that agents provide to their private clients.

Disclaimer

Various organizations and individuals are mentioned or shown in images in this publication. Unless stated in writing otherwise, none of those organizations nor individuals have endorsed this publication or its author in any way. No mention or reference to others in this publication is meant to imply they have read nor even heard of this publication.

This is not a book of advice. Do not make any decisions or commitments based on this booklet. This booklet is intended to help you identify topics that you should consult a professional advisor for.

Although the information in this publication was believed to be accurate and up to date at time of publication, it is not guaranteed in any way nor to any extent. You must verify all data, organizational descriptions, and references to experts in this publication via your own independent information gathering.

Title/Copyrights Page

SUDDENLY Your Elderly Parent Can No Longer Live Alone!
Copyright: **Lee Alley**
Published: June 15, 2012
Publisher: **Lee Alley**
First Edition

From "*The Urgent Caregiver*" Series by Lee Alley, Ph.D.

Find out more about the author and upcoming books online at www.Promise-Living.org or @LeeAlley.

Made in the USA
San Bernardino, CA
31 August 2018